# THE BAPTISM WITH THE Holy Spirit

JARED A. LASKEY

*To all the seekers of Spirit and Truth:*

*May you enter the Spirit-empowered life through these pages, and draw closer to Jesus everyday.*

Copyright © 2023 by Jared A. Laskey

All rights reserved. No part of this book may be reproduced or used in any manner without written permission of the copyright owner except for the use of quotations in a book review.
For more information, inquire at info@firebornministries.com.

Unless otherwise indicated, Scripture quotations are from the ESV® Bible (The Holy Bible, English Standard Version®), copyright © 2001 by Crossway Bibles, a publishing ministry of Good News Publishers. Used by permission. All rights reserved.

Graphics + cover design by Jessica Toach

ISBN 979-8-9887829-0-2 (paperback)
979-8-9887829-1-9 (e-book)

www.firebornministries.com

# Contents

Foreword _____ 7

Introduction _____ 11

Chapter 1: Foundations to our Adventure _____ 15

Chapter 2: Personally Encounter the Holy Spirit _____ 21

Chapter 3: Jesus, the Baptizer with the Holy Spirit ____ 29

Chapter 4: Embracing the Baptism _____ 37

Chapter 5: Personal Encounters _____ 45

Chapter 6: Witnessing the Baptism _____ 53

Chapter 7: Evidence of the Baptism _____ 67

Chapter 8: Silenced Tongues _____ 75

Chapter 9: How to Receive _____ 79

Chapter 10: Now That You Are Baptized _____ 83

Next Steps _____ 89

Acknowledgments _____ 91

Resources _____ 95

## *Foreword*

Jesus said, "The thief does not come except to steal, and to kill, and to destroy. I have come that they may have life, and that they may have it more abundantly" (John 10:10 NKJV).

The "life" Jesus brings to us is the born again experience, where we receive forgiveness, eternal life and Christ as Lord. Our spirit is given a re-birth and made to be a new creation.

The life that is more abundant is not a life of abundant belongings. Jesus said, "Watch out! Be on your guard against all kinds of greed; life does not consist in an abundance of possessions" (Luke 12:15 NIV). People can have millions or even billions of dollars and all the possessions money can buy, but they can be devoid of peace and live as lost souls one heartbeat away from an eternity in hell.

So just what is the abundant life Jesus spoke of? It is a life filled with the Holy Spirit, led by the Holy Spirit, a life in constant fellowship with the Holy Spirit, anointed by the

Holy Spirit, and used by the Holy Spirit in his miraculous love, power and wisdom.

What a delightful life this is! How meaningful it is! How eternally significant it is!

Jared Laskey is one of those people who delights in the Jesus style of abundant life. He is anointed and called by God to help people give themselves over to life in the Holy Spirit.

When I pastored a church for the last time, I hired Jared to be a youth leader. His youth services featured an emphasis on the Holy Spirit. Teens came not for secular entertainment, but for encounters with God.

In my fifty plus years of full time ministry, I have been a lead pastor for twenty-five of those years and have employed many youth pastors. Of all those, Jared stood out as the one most in love with the Holy Spirit, the one most enthused about being intimate with the Holy Spirit, and the one with the most faith to lead others into this intimacy.

As a young lead pastor I once asked the Lord, "What will my greatest achievement be?" I named off some things I had done and was doing. I felt God impress these words into my Spirit: "Your greatest achievement will probably be someone you encourage who will do greater things than you will ever do." Since then, I've endeavored to be the best possible encourager. It comforts me to hear Jared credit me with having encouraged him in the early days of his wonderful ministry. I'm delighted to recommend his book to you, but not just his book. I recommend his love of the Holy Spirit.

Jesus truly wants to give you, the reader, spiritual life and then give to you such a Spirit baptism that your life will continually overflow with abundant life — meaning intimate fellowship with the Holy Spirit.

In Christ's affection,

Wes Daughenbaugh
www.EncouragementExpert.com

## *Introduction*

Welcome to this book on the baptism with the Holy Spirit, an amazing encounter that I am thrilled to share with you. Whether you desire to receive this incredible empowerment or are simply curious to learn more about this biblical truth, you've come to the right place!

In this book, I aim to take a different approach from the typical discussions on this topic. Despite holding a couple of seminary degrees, my intention is not to provide dry reading or delve into deep theological treatises. Although there is a time and place for that, this book will be decidedly practical.

My goal is to activate you to receive the promised gift of the Holy Spirit. We will explore scriptural references, hear testimonies from individuals who have experienced Spirit baptism, and engage in prayer and activation exercises to facilitate your personal encounter.

By faith I believe that as you read through and complete this book, you will apply these teachings to your life and be baptized with the Holy Spirit!

Jesus, the baptizer with the Holy Spirit, longs to empower you. This authority is not limited to a select few but is available to all of His children. Today, He desires to equip you to be a more effective witness in proclaiming and demonstrating the love of Jesus.

During His earthly ministry, Jesus promised the coming of the Holy Spirit. In Luke 11:13, He assured us that if we ask for the Holy Spirit, we will receive Him. Our Heavenly Father, being generous and loving, delights in giving good gifts to His children. When God makes promises, He faithfully fulfills them.

When I was 18 years old, the baptism with the Holy Spirit radically transformed my life, propelling me to walk closer with Jesus. Although I was already a new, born-again Christian, growing in my relationship with God and in discipleship, receiving the baptism with the Spirit was a pivotal moment that brought about a complete and profound change within me. Describing the experience scarcely does justice to its incredible nature.

And just as it happened for me, it can happen for you, too.

On the Day of Pentecost, when the Holy Spirit was initially poured out upon the disciples, Peter declared in Acts 2:38-39 that everyone who believes will receive the gift of the Holy Spirit. This promise extends to you, your children, and all who are far off — every person whom the Lord our God calls to Himself.

The baptism with the Holy Spirit ushers you into a Spirit-empowered life. Despite the challenges in life, the Holy Spirit remains with you, working powerfully through you. He dwells within you, rests upon you, and surrounds you. When you are baptized with the Holy Spirit, you will be drawn closer to Jesus, regardless of the circumstances you may face.

This empowerment is not just for you but also for your friends, family, and church. According to Scripture, God promised it to all who call upon the name of the Lord.

Are you ready? Do you yearn for more of God and a personal encounter of the baptism with the Holy Spirit? Get ready to dive in as you pursue Him and His presence! Prepare yourself for an incredible adventure in the Spirit.

*Chapter I*

# Foundations to our Adventure into the Baptism with the Holy Spirit

Welcome, my fellow adventurers in the Spirit! I am thrilled to embark on this journey with you as we explore the scriptural reality of the baptism with the Holy Spirit. Whether you are here to receive the empowering touch of the Spirit, satisfy your curiosity or deepen your walk with God, I am here to guide you.

Before we dive into our study, it is crucial that we approach the Scriptures with open hearts and fresh eyes. Set aside any preconceived notions, biases or doctrinal prejudices. Our goal is to receive divine revelation, unencumbered by our past experiences or beliefs. Are you ready to approach the Word of God with humility and excitement? Let us surrender to the leading of the Holy Spirit and embark on this transformative journey together.

## Inviting the Holy Spirit

Pause for a moment and invite the person of the Holy Spirit to join you as you read this book. Picture Him filling the room, surrounding you and dwelling within you.

Speak these words aloud: *"Welcome, Holy Spirit. Thank You for being with me. As I read this book, I invite You to speak to me and fill me with Your presence. Draw me closer to Jesus through this encounter. In Jesus' name, I love You. Fill me now."*

Take a deep breath and feel the refreshing presence of the Holy Spirit. Now, let us resume our study with renewed anticipation.

## The Scripture: Truth and Life

The Scriptures are not mere words on a page; they are alive and filled with truth. Every word has been divinely inspired by the Holy Spirit, the breath of God Himself. In *The Passion Translation*, 2 Timothy 3:16-17 beautifully captures the empowering nature of Scripture: "Every Scripture has been written by the Holy Spirit, the breath of God. It will empower you by its instruction and correction, giving you the strength to take the right direction and lead you deeper into the path of godliness. Then you will be God's servant, fully mature and perfectly prepared to fulfill any assignment God gives you."

We can take heart in knowing that the Scriptures are God's words to us. We can picture them as love letters from our Creator, passed down from generation to generation, standing the test of time. Although it has been attacked, ridiculed, burned or litigated against, the Bible remains constant. Nations rise and fall, but the Scriptures have withstood everything. And its contents are not just moral and ethical, but true and right and good.

The Scriptures are to be read, studied, memorized and applied to our lives. They give us life and show us how to live in the abundance and overflow of life in the Spirit. The stories are true, and science, archaeology, geology and more are constantly proving and affirming that Scriptural records are true historical records and narratives. Not only that, for the last 2,000 years hundreds of millions of people have testified to the transformative work and power of the Holy Spirit in their lives in almost all cultures. The Spirit pours Himself out upon hungry hearts seeking for more of Him in their lives!

### Jesus, Our Teacher

Our Lord Jesus Christ assured His disciples that the Holy Spirit would teach them all things and bring to their remembrance everything He had said to them. The Spirit would be their constant companion, guiding them in truth. Jesus recognized the importance of prayer and its connection to the miraculous works they witnessed. In John 14:26 He said, "But the Helper, the Holy Spirit, whom the Father will send in my name, He will teach you all things and bring to your remembrance all that I have said to you." Through the Holy Spirit, the disciples would receive divine instruction and be empowered to continue the ministry of Jesus.

### Knowing the Holy Spirit

We must not only acknowledge the Holy Spirit as the divine author of Scripture but also seek to know Him personally. He is not an abstract concept nor is He distant, but He is a relatable and intimate part of the triune God. The Holy Spirit has emotions, a will, roles, work, thoughts and a distinct personality. Scripture refers to Him by various names and attributes, including the Spirit of Jesus, Spirit of Christ and Spirit of Truth. As 2 Corinthians 3:17 reminds us,

"Now the Lord is the Spirit, and where the Spirit of the Lord is, there is freedom."

It is important to know that the Scriptures are truth and life. In the book of Acts, Jesus sent His Spirit to empower the disciples to continue His ministry which we now have become part of. But most importantly, you and I can personally know the Holy Spirit just as they did. Before discussing Spirit baptism, I want you to understand that you can know the Spirit of God as a friend, personally and intimately.

### *Activation*:

Meditate on these words for ten minutes in silence and stillness: *"I can know the Holy Spirit personally and intimately. The Lord is the Spirit, and where the Spirit of the Lord is, there is freedom."*

*Chapter 2*

# Personally Encounter the Holy Spirit

You can personally encounter the Holy Spirit. Growing up in a Christian church, I had a solid Scriptural foundation, but I lacked a personal experience and relationship with the Spirit of God. It wasn't until I earnestly sought more of the Lord and received the precious baptism with the Holy Spirit that I truly began to understand we can worship the Holy Spirit.

I vividly remember the day of my Spirit-filling experience. It happened while I was attending Youth With a Mission's Discipleship Training School in Kona, Hawaii on November 14, 1998. In that transformative moment as I spoke in tongues for the first time, I couldn't help but worship the Spirit. For hours I switched between tongues and English, expressing my gratitude, praise, honor and worship to God the Father, God the Son and God the Holy Spirit. Afterwards, I wanted to tell everyone what happened to me, including an extremely educated and intelligent homeless agnostic man at Barnes and Noble!

Looking back now, I cannot help but laugh at my youthful zeal, but I am forever grateful for my baptism with the Spirit. I believe that He smiles and laughs with us as He accepts our childlike faith and our complete reliance on Him alone. Since that life-altering day, my fellowship and worship of the Spirit have deepened. I have had good days and bad days, rough years and blessed years. But He has always been with me.

The concept of worshiping the Holy Spirit may be new to you or even quite shocking. But I want to establish a biblical foundation for worshiping the Holy Spirit. However, before we delve into worshiping Him, let's understand a few key aspects about Him.

### Holy is Part of His Name

The Holy Spirit is holy. The word "holy" is part of His very name. It signifies being sacred, deserving of complete devotion, consecrated and set apart. Holiness is inherent in His nature. The *Holman Bible Dictionary* provides four distinct meanings of "holy."

First, it means to be "set apart," applying to places, things and persons connected to God or His holy places. Second, it represents perfection, transcendence and spiritual purity that evokes adoration and reverence. Third, it conveys a sense of awe, being beyond comprehension and inspiring fear. Lastly, it denotes being filled with supernatural power. A saint is a holy person, and to be sanctified is to be made holy.

When we encounter the term "Holy Spirit" in Acts 1:8, the original language reveals that "Holy Spirit" refers to something sacred, holy and set apart by or for God. The word "Spirit" signifies breath, wind, or Spirit (with a capital S). The context determines the intended meaning, and in Acts 1:8 it specifically refers to the person of the Spirit and not merely a wind or breath with little significance.

Living in a world filled with conflicting viewpoints, ideologies and diverse religious and spiritual practices, it becomes crucial for us, as Christians, to remain true to the Bible and to honor the Spirit who leads us into all truth and glorifies Jesus.

## The Primary Role of the Holy Spirit

One of the primary roles of the Holy Spirit is to glorify Jesus and make Him known to us. In John 15:26, Jesus said, "But when the Helper comes, whom I will send to you from the Father, the Spirit of truth, who proceeds from the Father, he will bear witness about me." The Spirit delights in glorifying Jesus. As Jesus stated in John 16:14, "He will glorify me, for he will take what is mine and declare it to you." This truth is worth meditating on.

Have you ever had a close friend whom you wanted to see succeed? You would go above and beyond to support them, lift them up and celebrate their progress and achievements. You would take joy in seeing their name recognized and honored. In a similar way, the Holy Spirit desires to see Jesus exalted, magnified, and celebrated in our lives and through our worship.

As followers of Christ, we are called to shift our focus from ourselves and our desires to pursue Jesus through the Holy Spirit. The Spirit works within us, convicting us of sin and leading us into righteousness. It is by the Spirit's power and guidance that we are transformed and made more like Jesus. Galatians 5:16 encourages us, saying, "But I say, walk by the Spirit, and you will not gratify the desires of the flesh." Through a surrendered life to the Spirit, we can live victoriously over sin and become vessels of God's holiness. He leads and guides us to know Jesus more.

## Honoring the Holy Spirit

Honoring the Holy Spirit involves recognizing His presence, acknowledging His ministry and inviting Him to work in and through us. King David, a man after God's own heart, provides us with an example of honoring the Spirit. After his sin with Bathsheba, he repented and pleaded with God saying, "Create in me a clean heart, O God, and renew a right spirit within me. Cast me not away from your presence, and take not your Holy Spirit from me" (Psalm 51:10-11). David understood the importance of the Spirit's presence and the need to honor Him.

Walking with the Spirit is a daily journey of surrender and reliance on Him. It is an ongoing process of aligning our will with God's will, submitting to His guidance and trusting His wisdom. As we walk with the Spirit we reflect Jesus' character, displaying the fruit of the Spirit in our lives. Love is the fruit of the Spirit, and the attributes of love are joy, peace, patience, kindness, goodness, faithfulness, gentleness and self-control. These traits become evident in our lives as we allow the Spirit to work within us.

Furthermore, obeying the Spirit is crucial in our walk with God. In Acts 10, we read about Peter's encounter with Cornelius, where the Spirit directed Peter to go and share the gospel with the Gentiles. Peter's obedience to the Spirit's leading opened the door for the expansion of the gospel to the Gentile nations. Just as Peter obeyed, we too must be willing to submit to the Spirit's guidance and direction, even if it takes us out of our comfort zones or challenges our preconceived notions.

### You Can Worship the Holy Spirit

If you are committed to the Lord, the Spirit now lives within you. The Holy Spirit has a personality, thoughts, emotions and more. Over time you can get to know Him, and you can fellowship with Him everyday (see 2 Cor. 13:14).

The Holy Spirit is God, and only God receives worship. Exodus 34:14 says, "Do not worship any other god, for the Lord, whose name is Jealous, is a jealous God" (NIV). God alone is worthy to be praised and worshiped. And we can worship each person in the Godhead: the Father, the Son and the Spirit.

The Spirit has all the same attributes, qualities and characteristics of God. He is eternal, all powerful, all knowing and present everywhere (see Hebrews 9:14, Psalm 139:7-16, and I Corinthians 2:1-16). In Him, He (the Spirit) glorifies Jesus, delighting in guiding us to Him. It is His joy to give us greater revelation and personal encounter with our heavenly Father and blessed Savior.

You can worship the Holy Spirit! It is of the utmost importance. The Spirit is God, worthy of our adoration, praise and worship. We can express our worship through our words, actions and relationships. It begins with an attitude of surrender, acknowledging His holiness, and inviting Him to have His way in our lives. So let us activate our faith and engage in personal worship of the Holy Spirit. He is waiting for us, eager to guide us into a deeper relationship with God and reveal more of Jesus to us. May our lives be a continual offering of worship to the precious Holy Spirit.

### *Activation:*

Worship the Holy Spirit directly. Play your favorite worship music, praising and worshiping the Spirit of God for the duration of three or more songs.

## Chapter 3

# Jesus, the Baptizer with the Holy Spirit

Let us turn our attention to the first reference to the baptism with the Holy Spirit, proclaimed by a man named John the Baptist. Clad in garments made from camel's hair and consuming a diet of locusts and wild honey, John seemed peculiar by most standards. Yet Jesus and many others recognized him as a prophet. He was the messenger preparing the way for the coming of the Lord, fulfilling prophecies from Isaiah and Malachi.

### John's Water Baptism and the Promise of Jesus

People from Jerusalem, Judea and the entire region of Jordan flocked to John to receive a water baptism of repentance, preparing their hearts for the Messiah's arrival. Many questioned John, wondering if he were the

Savior. In response, John humbly declared in Matthew 3:11-12, "I baptize you with water for repentance, but He who is coming after me is mightier than I, whose sandals I am not worthy to carry. He will baptize you with the Holy Spirit and fire." In the Gospel of Mark, John affirms that the One coming after him, the Savior, would baptize with the Holy Spirit.

One day, Jesus Himself approached John at the Jordan River in Israel. This encounter marked a holy moment for both John and Jesus. Astonished, John questioned why Jesus, the sinless Lamb of God, would seek water baptism from him. Jesus responded, "Let it be so now, for thus it is fitting for us to fulfill all righteousness" (Matt. 3:15). As Jesus emerged from the water, the heavens opened, and the Spirit of God descended upon Him in the form of a dove, while the voice of God proclaimed His pleasure in His beloved Son.

The following day, John testified about what he had witnessed, boldly proclaiming Jesus as the Lamb of God. He explained that God had revealed to him that the One on whom the Spirit descended and remained was the baptizer with the Holy Spirit.

## Jesus, the Baptizer with the Holy Spirit

As John the Baptist declared in Matthew 3:11-12, Mark 1:6-8, Luke 3:16-17 and John 1:32-34, Jesus is the baptizer with the Holy Spirit. John said, "...he who sent me to baptize with water said to me, 'He on whom you see the Spirit descend and remain, this is he who baptizes with the Holy Spirit.'"

Since the Day of Pentecost over two thousand years ago, Jesus has baptized people with the Spirit. In Acts 1:8 just before He ascended into Heaven, Jesus addressed a question from his disciples. They believed in a political restoration of the kingdom of Israel. But Jesus was having them think supernaturally, not upon a kingdom that comes and goes but a Kingdom that is eternal and spiritual. He said, "You will receive power when the Holy Spirit has come upon you, and you will be my witnesses in Jerusalem and in all Judea and Samaria, and to the ends of the earth" (Acts 1:8).

They obeyed and waited for the coming promise. In Luke 24:49 Jesus said, "I am going to send you what my Father has promised; but stay in the city until you have been clothed with power from on high" (NIV). The Holy Spirit would come upon them, equipping them for their mission on earth.

In John chapters 14, 15 and 16, Jesus elaborated on this promise, speaking about the coming of the Spirit. He assured His followers that the Holy Spirit would be their helper, the Spirit of Truth who would teach, guide and remind them of His words. Jesus wanted them to abide in His love, for the Holy Spirit would empower them and glorify Jesus in their lives.

This promise was not limited to the disciples alone. In Acts 2:38-39, Peter declared that the gift of the Holy Spirit was for everyone who called upon the name of the Lord. Jesus, the baptizer with the Holy Spirit, loves His children extravagantly. There is no measure to the love and empowerment He desires to bestow upon us.

Jesus was preparing His disciples' hearts for what He was about to send. They had no understanding of what to expect or what it would be like. But they waited in Jerusalem in the Upper Room, praying, fasting and expecting. In Luke 11, Jesus taught His disciples about prayer. They had observed the power and authority displayed in His life and recognized the connection between prayer and His miraculous works. Obediently, they prayed and waited. They were probably reminded by the Spirit what Jesus said, connecting prayer with receiving the Spirit.

When they asked Him to teach them how to pray, Jesus responded by contrasting the goodness of earthly parents, who give good gifts to their children, with the heavenly Father's infinite generosity. He assured them, "How much more will the heavenly Father give the Holy Spirit to those who ask Him!" (Luke 11:13). Now they were expecting the Holy Spirit and the promise of power as they prayed in the Upper Room.

Jesus answered their prayers and fulfilled His promise. As the baptizer with the Holy Spirit, the power of God fell upon them. And the world would never be the same.

Acts 2:1-4 says, "When the Day of Pentecost came, they were all together in one place. Suddenly a sound like the blowing of a violent wind came from heaven and filled the whole house where they were sitting. They saw what seemed to be tongues of fire that separated and came to rest on each of them. All of them were filled with the Holy Spirit and began to speak in other tongues as the Spirit enabled them" (NIV).

People from various corners of the world were present in the city celebrating the Feast of Pentecost. They heard the 120 disciples, now empowered by the Spirit, speaking in the languages of those gathered, knowing that these followers of Jesus did not know the languages previously. Those gathered said, "We hear them declaring the wonders of God in our own tongues!" (Acts 2:11 NIV). And through this supernatural sign, 3,000 people came to Jesus in one day. It was the first day of the Christian church.

Jesus came in power, as the baptizer with the Holy Spirit. The disciples, now empowered by the Holy Spirit, would go on to change the world as they testified about Jesus. And He wants to empower you, too!

The baptism with the Holy Spirit launches you into a lifelong journey of empowerment, intimacy and transformation. Embrace the reality that Jesus, the baptizer with the Holy Spirit, desires to fill you with His presence and power. Pursue a life infused with the Holy Spirit's power and love.

### _Activation_:

Let us pray together, embracing the promise of the baptism with the Holy Spirit. Pray this outloud: _"Lord Jesus, thank You for being the baptizer with the Holy Spirit. I am grateful for Your promise to give the Holy Spirit to those who ask. Today, I ask You to baptize me afresh with the Holy Spirit and fire. Fill me to overflowing, empowering me to walk in the fullness of Your Spirit. I surrender my life to You, Holy Spirit, and invite You to lead and guide me. In Jesus' name, amen."_

Now, take a few moments to rest in the presence of the Holy Spirit. Be expectant and open to His touch, His voice and His leading. Allow Him to minister to you in a personal and powerful way.

*Chapter 4*

# Embracing the Baptism with the Holy Spirit

In this chapter, we will delve deeper into the purpose of the baptism with the Holy Spirit, Jesus' role in it and the signs or evidence of Spirit baptism.

Luke, the physician and occasional companion of the Apostle Paul, begins the book of Acts by stating, "In the first book, O Theophilus, I have dealt with all that Jesus began to do and teach, until the day when he was taken up, after he had given commands through the Holy Spirit to the apostles whom he had chosen. He presented himself alive to them after his suffering by many proofs, appearing to them during forty days and speaking about the kingdom of God. And while staying with them he ordered them not to depart from Jerusalem, but to wait for the promise of the Father, which, he said, 'you heard from me; for John baptized with water, but you will be baptized with the Holy Spirit not many days from now'" (Acts 1:1-5).

Let's focus on the latter part of this passage: *"John baptized with water, but you will be baptized with the Holy Spirit."* John the Baptist proclaimed that Jesus is the baptizer with the Holy Spirit, and Jesus Himself promised it. Next, He affirmed that it was imminent. Just as John immersed people in water, the baptism with the Spirit would be an immersion. Though no one knew exactly what it would look like or when it would happen, the promise was on its way — a powerful baptism with the Holy Spirit, a spiritual and supernatural immersion of power by Jesus.

In Acts 2:33, the Apostle Peter, empowered by the Holy Spirit, proclaimed about Jesus, "Being therefore exalted at the right hand of God, and having received from the Father the promise of the Holy Spirit, he has poured out this that you yourselves are seeing and hearing." Jesus fulfilled the promise and poured out the Holy Spirit on the Day of Pentecost. From that point forward, He continues to pour out the baptism with the Spirit, faithfully keeping His word.

## The Purpose of Spirit Baptism

One of the primary purposes of the baptism with the Holy Spirit is to empower us to be witnesses for Jesus — to tell and show others who He is. As Acts 1:8 states, "You will receive power when the Holy Spirit has come upon you, and you will be my witnesses in Jerusalem and in all Judea and Samaria, and to the end of the earth."

The Greek word used for power in this verse is *dunamis* which means "miraculous power, might, strength, or ability." It is the power to perform marvelous works, to have efficacy and energy. Interestingly, this word appears 120 times in the New Testament, and it is worth noting that 120 people were present in the Upper Room on the Day of Pentecost.

The power bestowed in the baptism with the Spirit is the power of the Lord's ability working through us. It empowers us to walk with Him, to grow in becoming more like Him and to carry out His work. Jesus stated that His followers would do even greater things in His name when the Holy Spirit was present — all for His glory.

When we receive the baptism with the Spirit, we are infused with power to proclaim Jesus to others, to demonstrate His love, power, and grace and perform miracles. This power enables us to shine brighter in our homes, workplaces, schools and wherever we go. The Holy Spirit equips us to be more effective witnesses of Jesus and empowers us to live out the abundant life He promised.

However, it's essential to recognize the underlying foundation needed to fulfill this purpose: love for God and love for others. The baptism with the Spirit is not merely about receiving power; it is about glorifying Jesus, and living empowered to tell others about Him everywhere.

It is crucial to have His love in our hearts at all times. And it is always important to cultivate love for Him and for people. Without love, it becomes a supernatural experience that fails to transform us. Therefore, it is critically important to be rooted and grounded in His love and to invest time in daily relationship with Him. We must have His love in our hearts as we ask Him to baptize us with His Holy Spirit.

### The Signs of Being Baptized with the Spirit

The first sign of being baptized with the Spirit is love — the fruit of the Spirit. As Galatians 5:22-23 states, "But the fruit of the Spirit is love..." Love is the foundational fruit, and from it flows other attributes listed as joy, peace, patience, kindness, goodness, faithfulness, gentleness and self-control.

As Spirit-baptized followers of Jesus, it is vital for us to exhibit the signs or evidence of love for God and love for others. Our lives should reflect joy, peace, gentleness, kindness, and all the attributes of the fruit of the Spirit. Therefore, when seeking and asking for the baptism with the Holy Spirit, we need to search our hearts for love and commit our lives to demonstrate and walk in God's love. Our love should be towards God and then to others.

Apart from love, there are additional signs of the baptism with the Holy Spirit as witnessed in the book of Acts. In the second chapter regarding the initial outpouring of the Spirit, those gathered heard the sound of a mighty rushing wind and witnessed divided tongues of fire resting on each of them. They were filled with the Holy Spirit and began speaking in tongues as the Spirit gave them utterance.

When the disciples received the baptism with the Spirit on the Day of Pentecost, they spoke in languages that were understood by people from various regions. Empowered by the Spirit, they went out into the streets, preaching the gospel and praising God. Many people from different parts of the world understood their message and 3000 individuals surrendered their lives to Jesus that day, witnessing the signs of the baptism with the Spirit. As Peter stated in Acts 2:33, Jesus "poured out this that you yourselves are seeing and hearing."

Speaking in tongues, enabled by the Holy Spirit, is an evidence or sign of the baptism with the Holy Spirit. It refers to speaking in a language that the person does not know but is given by the power of the Spirit. This language can be spiritual or a spoken language on earth, unknown to the speaker personally. It helps us communicate spirit to Spirit. I've heard it described as being like a direct hotline between you and God. Some refer to speaking in tongues as a prayer language or spiritual language. But speaking in tongues was evident with the baptism with the Holy Spirit in Acts chapters 2, 10 and 19.

A pastor I served under had been preaching on this, and he mentioned that some people ask if they have to speak in tongues when they receive the Spirit baptism. He continued by saying, "You don't have to, but you get to!" It's a special privilege and precious gift that you are able to receive. The Apostle Paul said in I Corinthians 14:4 that speaking in tongues edifies the speaker. The New Living Translation says, "A person who speaks in tongues is strengthened personally..." and the English Standard Version states, "The one who speaks in a tongue builds up himself..."

Speaking in tongues edifies your spirit, building you up in faith and strengthening you for what life has to bring your way. It is direct access from your spirit through the Holy Spirit to God!

It is important to emphasize that the baptism with the Holy Spirit is for every believer, an outpouring of God's love. As the Apostle Peter declared in Acts 2:39, "The promise of the gift of the Spirit is for you, your children, and all who are far off — everyone whom the Lord our God calls.

### *Activation:*

Read I Corinthians 13 slowly four times through while listening to soft worship music.

Then pray this out loud: *"Jesus, I thank You for Your promise to give the gift of the Holy Spirit to all who call on Your name. Thank You for Your love, and may it flow through me. Thank You for the signs and evidence of the baptism with the Spirit. May I be rooted and firmly grounded in love for You and love for others. Holy Spirit, baptize me. Jesus, immerse me in love and power. In Jesus' name, amen."*

*Chapter 5*

# Personal Encounters with the Holy Spirit

In this chapter, I want to share some personal experiences of how individuals, including me and my wife, have received the baptism with the Holy Spirit. These encounters have been unique and transformative, and I believe they will inspire and uplift your faith.

### The Holy Spirit's Work in the Lives of the Disciples

Before we delve into personal testimonies, let us briefly review how the disciples received the baptism with the Holy Spirit. In Acts 2:1-5 on the Day of Pentecost, the disciples were gathered together when suddenly a sound like a rushing wind filled the house. Divided tongues of fire appeared, and they were all filled with the Holy Spirit, speaking in tongues as the Spirit enabled them.

Another significant moment occurred in Acts 10:44-46 when Peter was preaching to a group of Gentiles. As he spoke, the Holy Spirit fell on them, and they began speaking in tongues, astonishing the believers from among the circumcised.

Speaking in tongues and prophesying were evident manifestations when people received the baptism with the Spirit, as seen in these passages.

### How My Wife Received the Baptism with the Holy Spirit

My wife Rochelle received the baptism with the Holy Spirit when she was ten years old during a summer camp altar call. The speaker that night taught about Spirit baptism, and she responded to the invitation, coming forward with other campers who felt the drawing of the Spirit within them.

As she prayed and sought to receive, the speaker laid hands on her. In that moment, she saw spiritual words in her mind and spoke them out, experiencing a powerful encounter. Overwhelmed, she was "slain in the Spirit" and continued praying in tongues while lying on the ground. As she prayed, she felt God's love surrounding her, like waves of electricity, transforming her from within. After about thirty minutes, she stood up, completely changed and on fire for Jesus.

A few years later, she received a call from God to go to a specific Bible college, where we eventually met in the year 2000. Since then she has used her gifts and talents in music, leading people in worship through her beautiful voice and excellent piano skills.

### How I Received the Baptism with the Holy Spirit

I was eighteen years old and a student at the Youth With A Mission (YWAM) Discipleship Training School in Kona, Hawaii. I had quit drugs the day I flew to the school, and God was working deeply within me in the program as I pursued Him desperately. The fog of addiction had recently vanished, and I was praying and asking for "more" of God. I honestly didn't know what "more" of God meant, even though we sang songs about it. But I craved His presence and read anything I could about Him, absorbing all the teaching and services offered.

One day we were on work duties, and I overheard some international students talking in their native language and

I said, "I wish I could speak another language." Just then a woman from New Zealand asked me, "Do you speak in tongues?"

"No," I answered.

Immediately, she laid hands on my cheeks and prayed for me to receive the gift of tongues and encouraged me to ask for it in prayer. I didn't know fully what tongues and other spiritual gifts were, but I thought if that was the "more" I was asking for, then I wanted it. I read through most of the New Testament nightly and saw it in the scripture, but I was never taught about it and had not seen it before. I had supernatural dreams since I was a young boy, and it was through a series of dreams that I knew I needed to get right with God. This led me to YWAM, but I had little instruction on spiritual gifts or the baptism with the Holy Spirit.

Later that day my cheeks were on fire, and I had vivid dreams from God. My roommates told me the next morning after the missionary from New Zealand prayed over me that while I slept, my cheeks were a fiery red. They knew God was doing something in me. I was excited and hungry for more of God, diving into prayer and spiritual habits. I was on an adventure with Him, and over the course of a few weeks He spoke to me through visions, dreams and prophetic utterances through other people. I asked as many people as I could about spiritual gifts, and I asked for tongues each time I prayed.

Then on the night of November 14, 1998 I went to Sam, who was my small group leader, and explained everything God had been telling me during those weeks and how I was asking for tongues.

He listened and then asked, "So you want tongues?"

I answered, "Yeah, whatever that is."

He replied, "I believe God will give it to you now." He then told me to stand up, lift my hands and ask for the spiritual gift of tongues. He explained that the Holy Spirit might speak to me or show me a word or phrase in a language I didn't know, and he said I was to speak out the word or phrase the Holy Spirit gave me, repeating it and receiving more. I was excited, and in my mind I quickly asked God to forgive me of any sin. Sam then laid hands on me in prayer and I prayed out loud, "God, will you give me tongues, in Jesus' name?"

In an instant, the Spirit of God gave me a single word in tongues to speak out, and as I repeated it, more words erupted through me. The power of the wonderful Holy Spirit enveloped me as what seemed like waves of electricity and God's love and power washed over me. It seemed as though a spotlight exploded out of my mouth as I spoke in tongues, with my arms and hands surging with tremendous currents as the waves of power washed over the rest of my body. I loudly spoke in tongues, feeling immersed in His Spirit.

Over the course of several hours, there were three huge waves of power with many smaller waves in between. As one large wave ebbed away, Sam had me thank God in English and then ask for more. Each time I asked for more, additional words in tongues emerged. My prayer for "more of God" was answered as I laughed, cried and worshiped Jesus, the baptizer in the Holy Spirit.

A journal entry from that night sheds a little more light on my encounter but also reveals my youthfulness and vocabulary from the drug culture I recently left.

*"It was so amazing, so indescribable...I was shaking and focusing and began to speak and almost fell over so Sam sat me down, and my body was so gone if that makes sense. My mind was going out of my mouth which was moving and speaking, yet I controlled it. My arms were tingling and I wanted so much more; the second and third flows were the most amazing."*

I was truly transformed that night.

Sam told me to pray in tongues every day, which became a personal conviction of mine. After this encounter with the Holy Spirit, I had a boldness to share the gospel, a spiritual hunger for His power and a commission to lead others to Him.

I have seen many people baptized with the Holy Spirit over the years, with each person's encounter being unique and special. It is always awe-inspiring to see Jesus baptize them in His Spirit. Some people speak in tongues for the first time for less than a minute while others go longer. Some may feel power surge through them, while other people feel nothing.

There are some who need the laying on of hands for an increase of faith and agreement in prayer, and others who go to their prayer closet and report to me later how God baptized them with His precious Spirit without anyone else present. I have asked myself why this is the case, having no solid answer besides the experience being scriptural truth. I think God gives each of us the Spirit baptism in the way we personally need to receive it. Each story is incredible, and I love seeing God answer every individual's prayer for "more."

In Luke 11:13 Jesus said, "If you then...know how to give good gifts to your children, how much more will the heavenly Father give the Holy Spirit to those who ask Him!" If you want more of God in your life, or if you want to receive the incredible baptism with the Holy Spirit and speak in tongues simply ask, knowing that He will answer by blessing you and giving you more of Him because He is a great Father who loves you.

### *Activation:*

Picture Jesus laying His hands on you and baptizing you with His Holy Spirit. Write in your prayer journal what you are expecting Him to do and what you sense Him doing in these moments.

*Chapter 6*

# Witnessing the Baptism with the Holy Spirit

Throughout my years in ministry, the Holy Spirit and His empowerment have remained central to my work, life and ministry. It has been a privilege to witness thousands of individuals receive the baptism with the Holy Spirit in various ways, and in differing places and situations.

When I first embarked on my ministry journey, I would gather a group of people to lay hands on those seeking Spirit baptism. As the person in need of prayer fervently sought and praised God, everyone in the group would pray aloud in tongues. It was truly remarkable to witness as new vowels, syllables and even words in an unknown language flowed from their mouths. They were receiving the precious gift of speaking in tongues. The manifestations varied from person to person — some would shake, others would fall and pray in tongues. While some experienced this divine encounter for just a minute or two, others felt the power up to fifteen minutes or more. Each experience was unique, yet they all received the baptism with the precious Holy Spirit.

There have been countless instances where individuals received the Spirit baptism through my personal ministry. A key I have learned is that when people ask questions about the baptism with the Spirit, it is an opportunity for me to partner with the Holy Spirit and see Him do something amazing. This principle is also true when non-Christians ask about Jesus or the gospel. People may even be curious about healing, miracles, signs and wonders. All of those instances become an invitation to see Jesus work in power!

I recall the first occasion during which I prayed with a man and his wife without anybody else present. No group was there to lay hands on this man except me. They came to me after he rid his life and home of things the Spirit told him to get rid of, and he said he wanted to receive the baptism with the Holy Spirit.

I mentioned to him that he may "hear" in his spiritual ear a word or phrase in a language he doesn't understand or know. He also might "see" this word or phrase in his mind. Once he does, he needs to speak it out. There is oftentimes an initial word the Spirit gives a person as Jesus baptizes them in His Spirit. Usually when they start speaking it out loud, more words flow out in praise to God. It can go on for seconds, minutes or hours at a time depending on what the Holy Spirit is doing.

This young man prayed and I quietly prayed in tongues over him. He first started speaking out a word that the Holy Spirit gave him: *Tsidkenu*. He repeated this word over and over, and then other words flowed. As a Bible college student at the time, I knew one of the Hebrew names of God was Yahweh Tsidkenu or Jehovah Tsidkenu: The Lord our Righteousness. So this young man's first word in his prayer language — in tongues — was righteousness. The most amazing part was that he had never heard it before!

More recently, I had an extraordinary encounter with a man while working on a job site at a gun range. I could sense that the Spirit was about to fill him, as he had been inquiring about it persistently for a week. We prayed together outdoors, and the Spirit descended upon him. He began to shake under the power of God and soon started speaking in tongues. For him, it started with hearing a sound in the Spirit, and then once he spoke it out it became words.

More words in tongues flowed from him, and his overflowing joy prompted him to rush to his room to read the Bible and engage in further prayer. I encouraged him to pray in tongues daily, and witnessing his response filled me with awe. His newfound prayer language, coupled with his renewed enthusiasm for reading the scriptures and communing with God unmistakably displayed the signs of being baptized with the Spirit.

On a recent Spirit-empowered coaching call, I was talking to a woman in Mozambique. As we listened to the Holy Spirit, He led her to repent and renounce some things that were holding her back from the fullness of life in Christ. She then asked for the baptism with the Spirit. As we listened for the voice of the Holy Spirit to speak, she told me that she heard a sound. I explained to her that this sound, one she had never heard before, was the beginning of receiving tongues with the Spirit baptism.

She started speaking out the sound, and then a wave of the Holy Spirit fell upon her as Jesus baptized her. More sounds and words flowed as she laughed, cried and shook. It was truly a holy moment for one of His kids.

## Receiving the Spirit Baptism in a Children's Home

For a few years after graduating Bible college, I worked at a residential foster treatment facility and school. The kids who lived there had multiple diagnoses stemming from trauma and abandonment. I had made a habit of praying in tongues around them. These kids heard everything and would be curious. Remember that I said when people ask you a question about spiritual things, it's an invitation to see God do something amazing?

Well, the kids would ask and I would tell them it was a prayer language Jesus gives. One night I had a group of seven kids in the living room while others were watching a movie. One boy asked how he could have this language. Then a few of the others chimed in and said they would like this language, too. I quickly told them an age-appropriate version of what the baptism of the Spirit entailed, but knew I might get in trouble from other staff if I was seen laying hands on them. (They were all living at the treatment home due to traumatic experiences so physical touch wasn't always allowed or welcomed.)

All the kids in the room wanted to pray to receive, so I led them in a prayer asking Jesus to baptize them with the Holy Spirit in Jesus' name. Next I felt a wind over my right shoulder which flew over the three kids on my right, and they started speaking in tongues! Then the wind went up to the kid in the middle and he was filled up, and finally it went back down to my left and swept over the other three kids. All seven kids were speaking in tongues for the next half hour. I was shocked and amazed, and I praised God!

After I put the kids to bed, I called a long term staff member (who was also a believer) about the night's events, and he advised me to simply tell the truth if any other staff brought it up. It was very straightforward: they prayed, God moved. No one on staff ever asked me about it, and within the course of a year I saw over twenty additional kids receive the baptism with the Spirit at the treatment facility. It was incredible to watch a genuine move of God take place with kids who had already been through so much difficulty in life.

### Remotely Receiving Spirit Baptism

My wife and I put together a short e-course called "*The Baptism with the Holy Spirit*" which is available on my ministry's website and on Charisma Magazine's e-course website. The principles shared are biblical, and we pray for people by faith to have Jesus baptize them in the Spirit as He falls upon them. We have had over 2000 students to date go through the e-course and participate in the prayer of activation. All glory to God!

A woman named Susan shared her testimony from her experience with the e-course.

*"I wanted you to know that I just completed your Baptism with the Holy Spirit free e-course. I received the Holy Spirit into my life, praise God! I followed along, prayed with you, in faith I asked Jesus to baptize me with the Holy Spirit, to come into my life and He did! I spoke in tongues for twenty to thirty minutes! I was like a babbling brook with a river of words coming out of my mouth so fast, and the Lord had control of my tongue! It was glorious! Praise God, thank you Jesus for this awesome grace gift!*

*I had been praying and asking for the baptism of the Holy Spirit for a few months and had not received it until now. I was raised in a Christian church and baptized at age twelve, born again at age 54 and now baptized with the Holy Spirit at age 62! I was never taught about the baptism of the Holy Spirit and the indwelling of God's power or about speaking in tongues.*

*During Covid lockdown, I wanted to press in and go deeper into the Bible and increase my faith. There were times when I could feel the presence of God in me, when I was praying, praising and worshiping. It felt like an electric current was going through my body. I heard Pentecostal pastors preach online and really liked what they were saying about what is happening in our world today. My church had gone silent and I decided to leave because I wasn't being fed or filled there spiritually.*

*I wanted to know the Holy Spirit; I wanted more. So I started reading books on the baptism of the Holy Spirit and really hungered to know God more. I am so glad that God led me to your video. I am honored to have received God's promise of this beautiful grace gift of His Holy Spirit.*

*Thank you for offering this free e-course. I have already ordered your Spirit-led journal. I'm praying in the Spirit every day, like you said."*

Her story is one of many we have seen in which Jesus baptizes people in the Spirit. Through the years I have seen people receive their baptism in the church van, sitting at coffee tables, over the phone or via online calls with me. After many years of this supernatural experience becoming a reality, praying for others to receive Spirit baptism comes easily for me. I simply have people focus on Jesus, worship and praise Him and then ask. We agree together in prayer in Jesus' name and wait expectantly for Jesus to baptize them with the Holy Spirit.

## How My Kids Received the Baptism with the Holy Spirit

My four children each received the baptism with the Holy Spirit through simple prayer. It was a truly remarkable experience for me as a parent, observing the Lord carry out His promise by filling them with His Spirit.

My oldest son Zechariah was five years old and came into my room when I was praying in tongues. He said he wanted to do what I was doing. So I explained to him that I was speaking in tongues, communicating with God. I then shared with him how God could give it to him, by speaking to his mind in words, syllables or phrases he had never spoken before. He needed to speak it out loud, as the Holy Spirit would give more words and phrases in tongues to say.

I laid hands on him in prayer, and he quickly received the Spirit baptism and spoke in tongues. It was a joyous occasion for me, and the entire process was so simple and sweet.

My twins were four years old, and I was putting them to bed. My wife and I would pray with our kids every night. On this night, I sensed the presence of God heavily on both Lydia and Malachi. I led them in a prayer asking Jesus to baptize them with the Holy Spirit, and then they received and spoke in tongues for quite a while. I told them to lay in bed and keep praying in tongues.

When my youngest son Isaiah was five years old, he came into my bedroom just like Zechariah had done years before. Isaiah overheard me praising God in my prayer language and he said, "I want to speak Spanish."

I laughed and replied, "It's not Spanish. It's my prayer language between me and God. Would you like God to give you a spiritual language to pray in?"

He said yes! Then I told him that Jesus is the one who baptizes in the Spirit, and when a word or phrase comes to mind he is to speak it out. Isaiah then put the blanket over his head, and after repeating a prayer asking Jesus to fill him with the Spirit, he started singing in tongues! I praised God with him as together we spoke in tongues.

## Holy Spirit Falling Upon or Through the Laying On of Hands

I have lost count of how many times I have encouraged people to pray at home while listening to worship music, asking God to fill them with His power. Remarkably, within an hour or so they would call or text me to share the news of their reception of the baptism with the Spirit. I have also heard incredible stories of people worshiping God while driving and suddenly find themselves praying in tongues.

I firmly believe that God administers this transformative experience according to His own will, and Jesus imparts it in a manner that is most receptive to the individual. As I mentioned earlier, we have had thousands of people take our free e-course on the baptism with the Holy Spirit and testify to Jesus baptizing them with His Spirit by falling upon them. What an amazing benefit of technology! Many others have received as we have laid hands on them in prayer as Jesus answers and immerses them in His power.

Within the Bible, there are two ways the baptism with the Holy Spirit is administered. It is through the laying on of hands in prayer and through the Spirit falling upon the recipients.

The first recorded instance of Spirit baptism was in Acts 2 when the Holy Spirit was poured out upon those in the Upper Room. This was fulfilling Jesus' promise in Acts 1:8 of the Spirit falling upon or coming upon them.

In Acts 10:44-46, the Spirit fell upon the household of Cornelius while the Apostle Peter was sharing the gospel message. The disciples with Peter saw and heard those in the house "speaking in tongues and praising God." Peter shared this testimony in Acts 11:15-18 saying, "The Holy Spirit came on them as He had on us at the beginning." (The *beginning* Peter is referencing is the Day of Pentecost in Acts 2.)

In Acts 8:17, it shows how Peter and John laid hands on new believers in Samaria, and the baptism with the Holy Spirit was both seen and heard. In Acts 9, Ananias was led by the Spirit to lay hands on Saul, so that he may receive his sight again and be filled with the Holy Spirit. Saul, later known as Paul, wrote in I Corinthians 14:18, "I thank God that I speak in tongues more than all of you." Accordingly, Paul must have received tongues in His Spirit baptism when Ananias laid hands on him in prayer.

Later in Acts 19:1-7, Paul laid hands on twelve believers in Ephesus. Verse six says, "When Paul had laid his hands on them, the Holy Spirit came on them, and they began speaking in tongues and prophesying."

You can receive the baptism with the Holy Spirit in either one of these two ways. Jesus wants to baptize you, fulfilling His promise to you because He loves you. And He will empower you to be an amazing witness for Him.

### *Activation*:

Read and study Acts chapters 2, 8, 10, 11 and 19. Put yourself in the biblical narrative as you read the accounts of Jesus baptizing people with His Spirit. Write down what it was like as you imagine yourself in the story. How did you see it, sense it or hear it? Then engage in a conversation with Jesus, thanking Him that He will baptize you with His Spirit.

**Chapter 7**

# Evidence of the Baptism with the Holy Spirit

As believers, we have the privilege of receiving as much of the Holy Spirit as we desire, considering that Jesus Himself was given the Spirit without measure. Moreover, since we possess the same Spirit that raised Jesus from the dead, our capacity to be filled by the Holy Spirit is limitless. This filling occurs when we surrender our lives to Jesus and enter into fellowship with Him. Through faith, we can continually experience and be filled with the Holy Spirit in various ways.

The baptism with the Holy Spirit is a biblical encounter that empowers us to become witnesses who are better equipped for Jesus. This is a significant one-time supernatural encounter with Jesus, the baptizer with the Spirit. This experience not only grants us power to be a bold witness for Jesus but also transforms us into the image of Christ. Our character should be continually shaped by the Holy Spirit on a daily basis, resulting in a life characterized by the fruit of the Spirit which is love. Love encompasses many attributes such as patience, kindness, goodness, faithfulness, gentleness and self-control, all of which flow from the singular fruit of the Spirit.

### Evidence of the Spirit Empowerment

Over the years, theologians and pastors have debated the terminology and vocabulary associated with the "evidence" of the Holy Spirit's baptism. My question is: *Shouldn't there be some form of proof when someone is filled with the Holy Spirit?*

The Bible indeed presents evidence of Spirit baptism, and speaking in tongues is one form of verification. It is something tangible, visible and audible that can indicate a person's baptism with the Spirit. However, there are other forms of evidence that I will discuss further.

According to the Merriam-Webster Dictionary, evidence can be defined as "an outward sign or indication, furnishing proof or testimony." In a legal sense, evidence is something presented to a court to establish the truth. When the Holy Spirit fills His children, there is visible evidence of His presence — a sign or proof of being filled.

While the legal definition of evidence may not directly apply, as believers in Christ, we are filled with the Spirit to bear witness about Him, to demonstrate His love and share the gospel with others. And there should be a sign to those around you that the Holy Spirit has baptized you.

### Speaking in Tongues

Acts 2:1-6 describes the events of the day of Pentecost, where the believers were gathered together in one place. Suddenly, there came from heaven a sound like a mighty rushing wind, filling the entire house, followed by divided tongues of fire resting upon each person. They were all filled with the Holy Spirit and began speaking in other tongues as the Spirit enabled them. At that time, there were Jews from different nations in Jerusalem for the feast of Pentecost, and they were astonished to hear the disciples speaking in their own languages.

The evident manifestation on the day of Pentecost was speaking in tongues, fulfilling the promise of the Father poured out through the baptism with the Holy Spirit. These tongues were actual spoken languages that the disciples did not know beforehand, and people from various nations heard and saw the evidence of the 120 believers being filled or baptized with the Spirit.

### Prophecy as Evidence

Acts 19:1-7 says, "And it happened that while Apollos was at Corinth, Paul passed through the inland country and came to Ephesus. There he found some disciples. And he said to them, 'Did you receive the Holy Spirit when you believed?' And they said, 'No, we have not even heard that there is a Holy Spirit.' And he said, 'Into what then were you baptized?' They said, 'Into John's baptism.' And Paul said, 'John baptized with the baptism of repentance, telling the people to believe in the one who was to come after him, that is, Jesus.' On hearing this, they were baptized in the name of the Lord Jesus. And when Paul had laid his hands on them, the Holy Spirit came on them, and they began speaking in tongues and prophesying. There were about twelve men in all."

This shows prophecy as evidence because they spoke in tongues and prophesied.

## Boldness in Preaching the Gospel

In Acts 4:31 after the believers had prayed, the place where they were gathered was shaken, and they were all filled with the Holy Spirit. As a result, they spoke the word of God with boldness. The evidence of being filled with the Spirit in this case was boldly proclaiming the word of God. When people are filled with the Spirit, one can observe and hear the evidence through their bold sharing of the gospel, even if it is uncharacteristic of their usual demeanor. Something significant has changed and transformed them. The Spirit empowers us to be witnesses to the power of the gospel message. Thus, speaking the gospel with boldness is evidence of being filled with the Spirit. This was clearly seen on the Day of Pentecost in Acts 2 and other accounts after the outpouring of the Holy Spirit.

## Wisdom and Wise Living

As the early Church expanded, there arose a need for delegation of tasks for acts of service. In Acts 6, we see how men of good reputation, full of the Spirit and wisdom, were appointed as the first deacons to serve the widows. Stephen, one of these chosen individuals, was described as being full of the Holy Spirit and wisdom. And the Holy Spirit is referred to as the "Spirit of wisdom and revelation" in Ephesians 1:17 by the Apostle Paul.

## Signs and Wonders

Examining Stephen more closely in Acts 6:8, we discover that he was not only full of grace and power but he also demonstrated signs and wonders. The power mentioned here refers to the same power of the Spirit described in Acts 1:8 — miraculous power, might and strength. Stephen's fullness of grace aligned with the kindness we find in the fruit of the Spirit mentioned in Galatians 5. As a result he walked in power, and signs and wonders occurred through him. Acts 6:8 states, "And Stephen, full of grace and power, was doing great wonders and signs among the people."

Boldly proclaiming the gospel, exhibiting wisdom and wise living, prophesying and demonstrating power through signs and wonders are all evidence to demonstrate being baptized with the Spirit, along with speaking in tongues. The Spirit baptism is the beginning or the entrance into the Spirit-empowered life!

As believers, after we receive the baptism with the Holy Spirit, we should seek to be continually filled. Ephesians 5:18 says, "And do not get drunk with wine, for that is debauchery, but be filled with the Spirit." This Bible verse is a command we are to obey by asking for continual fillings of the Spirit. We must always allow His presence to manifest in our lives and bear witness to the transformative work He accomplishes within us. Start today by asking for the baptism with the Holy Spirit!

### *Activation:*

Worship the Father, the Son and the Holy Spirit. Minister to each person of the Godhead for the next thirty minutes.

Then pray this prayer out loud: *"Father God, I obey Your Word and I ask to be filled continually with Your Holy Spirit. In the name of Jesus, fill me now. I receive everything you have for me, all spiritual gifts, enablements, power and wisdom. I surrender and yield to you now. May your evidence of the Spirit-empowered and Spirit-filled life be seen and heard, both in me and through me."*

*Chapter 8*

# Silenced Tongues

Perhaps you have already received the baptism with the Spirit in the past, but you have since ceased exercising this precious gift of speaking in tongues. You have what I will refer to as "silenced tongues." I want to assure you that the gift was given to you, and you simply need to activate it once again. You have already been baptized with the Spirit, but now it is time to be refilled and live a Spirit-empowered life. There is one baptism with the Spirit in our lives, but numerous fillings afterward as we are commanded in Ephesians 5:18 to be constantly filled with the Holy Spirit.

### How My Mom Spoke in Tongues Again

The first time my mom spoke in tongues, she had gone to bed with a prayer burden. During the night, she woke up spontaneously praying in tongues! Even though she recognized it as a supernatural experience, she soon dismissed it as a one-time event.

However, on a mission trip with me in the Dominican Republic I told her she still had tongues. I asked her to try remembering a phrase and speak it out. Just then a guy on a motorcycle was driving by, and his motorcycle died in front of us. My mom ministered to him and led him to commit his life to Jesus. Then his motorcycle started and he drove off into his new life. As my mom walked away, she prayed for him and it shifted to praying in tongues for him. She walked up to me and exclaimed, "It happened!"

### Rekindling the Gift of Tongues

During one of my *"Everyday Power Encounters"* seminars at a church, a woman and her husband approached me with a heartfelt story. She had previously received the gift of tongues but had been persuaded by other Christians, who were cessationists, that it was not from the Lord. Consequently, she had refrained from speaking in tongues for years, believing she committed the blasphemy of the Holy Spirit. I reassured her that she did not blaspheme the Spirit, and that He wanted to fill her again.

Her faith was being renewed through the teaching of God's Word in my seminar, and with her husband standing by her side, we laid hands on her. Immediately she began to remember some of the words she had spoken in tongues before.

As the Spirit descended upon her, tears of joy streamed down her face, accompanied by laughter and an overwhelming sense of love. She continued praying in tongues for about ten minutes and shared her testimony of receiving visions of people and nations. She had become an intercessor for the salvation of souls as her prayer language was reignited. Isn't that simply astounding?

If you find yourself in a similar situation where you stopped speaking in tongues, or fellow Christians convinced you it is not for today, just know that God loves you. And He wants you to know Him so much more. The gifts He gives, He doesn't take away. Scripture says that His gifts and call are irrevocable. You still have every spiritual gift He has given you. Tongues are still there; they have just been silent. Choose at this moment to speak them out.

Begin asking Jesus to fill you with His Holy Spirit. Start seeking, continue asking and then open yourself up to speak in tongues again. As you worship Jesus, remember in your mind some of the spiritual words and phrases in tongues you had spoken in the past. Then speak them out, worshiping and praising Jesus. Continue to pray in tongues daily, adding it to your devotional time, when you commute to work or go on walks.

*Chapter 9*

# How To Receive the Baptism with the Holy Spirit

Are you ready to receive the baptism with the Holy Spirit? You've made it this far so congratulate yourself! I want you to understand that the sequence of topics shared here are principles I have learned along the way in life and ministry. I do not recommend that this become a dogmatic or staunch method on how to receive the baptism with the Holy Spirit. Keep in mind that our God is creative and loves to bless each believer with a unique experience!

The Holy Spirit can fall upon you which is what you should expect as you apply the following principles. You can also have fellow believers lay hands on you and receive the promise of the Holy Spirit. Either way, approach Jesus like a child and ask Him to baptize you in His Holy Spirit. Ask expectantly for Him to give it to you because He will!

As you approach this time, fix your gaze upon Him and earnestly ask Him to baptize you with His precious Holy Spirit. Be receptive to His divine impartation as a syllable, phrase, or sound comes to your mind or spiritual ears. Speak it out repeatedly, allowing yourself to hear your own voice. Continue speaking in this spiritual language enabled by the Holy Spirit. You engage in the act of speaking while the Holy Spirit enables you. Let the power of God flow through you as you receive the baptism with the Spirit, regardless of how long the process takes. From that point forward, make it a habit to pray in this spiritual language daily.

Read through these steps and then start by playing some soft worship music, free from any distractions. Confess any sins as the Spirit brings them to your mind. If you are going through this with a Bible class, have a few spiritual leaders lay hands on you during this time. You can also have those who speak in tongues lay hands on you. Take your time as you worship Him and listen to His voice. Apply each step or have a leader share the steps as led by the Spirit.

1. <u>Worship Jesus</u>.
   Turn your heart and affections to Him.

2. <u>Ask Jesus to baptize you in the Holy Spirit</u>.
   He loves you so much. He said that if you ask for the Holy Spirit, He will give Him to you.

3. <u>Surrender to the Spirit of God</u>.
   When you surrender to the Spirit, He fills you. Tell the Holy Spirit you yield and surrender to Him. Let Him fall on you.

4. <u>Speak in tongues</u>.
   You may see in your mind or hear in your spiritual ears a language you have never spoken. Speak it out loudly enough to hear yourself and keep speaking it, continuing to worship Jesus. Allow more words to form and speak them out. Don't rush. This can take place in five seconds, two minutes or hours at a time. Ask for more and boldly speak in tongues.

5. <u>Be thankful</u>.
   Give God the glory and praise, thanking Him in your native language and in tongues.

6. <u>Pray in tongues daily</u>.

While you walk, drive or in your prayer closet, pray in your new heavenly language. The more you speak in tongues, the more the language will grow. Set aside time everyday to pray in tongues.

***Chapter 10***

# Now That You Are Baptized with the Holy Spirit

Now that you have received the baptism with the Holy Spirit, go and tell other people about Jesus. You are a Spirit-empowered believer because of the baptism with the Spirit. Share Jesus' love with others. And pray in tongues every day, growing your spiritual language.

Speaking in tongues is an amazing and precious gift. Many churches have tried to shy away from it, hiding it in the back room and leaving it only to intercessory prayer meetings or counseling sessions. Some leaders may apologize for praying in tongues even though it is a biblical truth.

Our faith needs to be rooted and established in love: love for God and love for others. It bears repeating that I

Corinthians 13 is known as the "love chapter." It is most often read at weddings. Even though it is a beautiful chapter, its context is referring to spiritual gifts and not marriage. This chapter was sandwiched in between chapters 12 and 14 which discuss the proper use of God's awesome spiritual gifts.

This love chapter describes what our attitude and motivation need to be in using spiritual gifts. Verses 8-10 say, "Love never fails. But where there are prophecies, they will cease; where there are tongues, they will be stilled; where there is knowledge, it will pass away. For we know in part and we prophesy in part, but when completeness comes, what is in part disappears." Some people refer to these verses, saying that spiritual gifts ceased and were only for the first century church. But as these verses say, spiritual gifts will cease when "that which is perfect comes."

While some might argue that "the perfect" refers to the completed canon of Scripture, rather it refers to Christ Himself since verse 12 says, "For now we see as through a glass, dimly, but then, face to face." Therefore, the spiritual gifts will cease only when Jesus returns or when our time here is finished.

Some believers may see this interpretation as a stretch, but if we take the entire context of the epistle of I Corinthians into consideration, this is hinted at in 1:7-8. Paul tells the Corinthians that he gives thanks for them "so that you are not lacking in any gift, as you wait for the revealing of our Lord Jesus Christ, who will sustain you to the end, guiltless in the day of our Lord Jesus Christ." That day is when He comes back for His Church.

The gift of tongues is an incredible spiritual gift. We must develop our spiritual language after Jesus gives it to us when we receive the baptism with the Holy Spirit (Matt. 3:11, Luke 3:16, Acts 1:8).

The apostle Paul is a great model for us to follow, as he taught that tongues were not a one time or occasional matter, but it was instead a lifestyle. In I Corinthians 14:18 he said, "I thank God that I speak in tongues more than you all." This should be the same in our lives and churches. This should not be just a summer camp experience or a special once-a-year church service. It should be applied to our daily lives.

Some people have come to me after a few weeks of their baptism with the Holy Spirit, and they seem discouraged. They are frustrated because they only repeat the same few words in tongues which they received when they were first filled with the Spirit. I reassure them that they are on the right track and need to continue in it. Their prayer language is about to grow.

I explain to them that when we were children, we grew our language through repetition. We learned words or phrases, adding them to our vocabulary little by little. Thus, as we pray and repeat the words or phrases in tongues the Holy Spirit gave us, our spiritual language will grow and develop. Whether we are driving, walking down the street or in our prayer closet, we should use every opportunity to pray in tongues.

As we pray in the tongues of men and angels, it is a process of time and growth (1 Cor. 13:1). And praying in tongues is personally edifying as Paul said, "The one who speaks in a tongue builds up himself" (1 Cor. 14:4). We should be excited that we pray, worship Him and build ourselves up through the gift of tongues. We are connecting with Him on a personal level in a supernatural way.

We should also sing in tongues in our times alone with God. I Corinthians 14:15 says, "I will pray with my spirit, but I will pray with my mind also; I will sing praise with my spirit, but I will sing with my mind also." This is a key to developing our spiritual language and in learning how to interpret them as we pray and sing in this gift. We can all do this at home by incorporating praying and singing in tongues during our personal time with God. Then we can ask God to give us the interpretation of what we just prayed and sang. As His wonderful Spirit gives us the interpretation, we should write it down in our journal and keep it between us and Him as we praise (1 Cor. 14:16).

May you continue to grow and develop in love toward God and others. And I pray your spiritual language soars to new heights as you draw near to Jesus.

### *Activation:*

Pray and sing in tongues for 30 minutes per day for the next seven days and record in your prayer journal what God does in you.

## *Next Steps*

Email us at <u>info@firebornministries.com</u> to share your story of what Jesus did in you through this book. Let us know how he baptized you with His Holy Spirit! We will celebrate with you and send you more resources as you enter into more of the Spirit-empowered life.

Connect with us on our social media!

   Fireborn Ministries

   @firebornministries

   Fireborn Ministries

*Enjoy your very own adventures in the Spirit!*

## *Acknowledgments*

I would like to say thank you to my lovely bride, Rochelle Laskey, for the adventure of 21 years of marriage at the time of this writing. For being supermom, an incredibly gifted musician and worshiper and for editing this short manuscript. I love you. To our kids, Zechariah, Lydia, Malachi and Isaiah; I love you with all my heart. You have all heard God since a young age. May you grow more in Him and teach your kids the principles your mom and I have taught you. And may the Laskey family keep traveling!

Thanks to my parents, Allen and Jeanette Laskey, for raising me on the word of God; even though I strayed as a teenager, the Holy Spirit got ahold of me in power. And to my in-laws, Dave and Rhonda Van Soelen, for the phone calls, birthday and holiday cards and Facetimes to check in on me.

Thanks to Joan Hunter for capturing a part of my story in her book, *Miracles for Veterans*. Thanks to the prophetic and apostolic voices over the years who are just a phone call away, Bob Laflin, John Natale, Elizabeth Tiam Fook, Tom Ruotolo, Kathy DeGraw, and Tom Stamman.

To Craig and Colette Toach and all the Next Gen Prophets, may more tribes like yours multiply around the world. To Jessica Toach for designing the book cover, thank you for using your gifts in excellence. And all the *Adventures in the Spirit with Jared Laskey* podcast guests such as Shawn Bolz, Jane Hamon, Bishop Bill Hamon, Patricia King, Tony Kim, Robby Dawkins, and the over 200+ guests. It's been an awesome ride!

Gratitude to Anne Verebely for giving me a chance to be a radio personality at Current FM. To the late Dr. Steve Greene for believing in me and speaking into my life no matter what you had going on; may the world follow your example of leading with love.

To my friends Scott and Lynn Gilbert for walking with me through God's transformation since 2018 and the Krav Maga lessons; to Don and Lisa Nash for your listening ear, spiritual hunger and humility; to Nick and Crystal Kupper for 'adopting' us as we moved to Arizona (though we've been friends for years) and your courageous commitment putting everything on the line and overcoming against all odds. To Randy and Lesli Bixby and the Family Reformation Project, standing and fighting for family and being transparent in your healing story. To Christina Perera, for your confirming prophetic words over the phone at a pivotal moment in my life this year, and Caleb Wampler's personal text messages giving me encouragement no matter what is taking place. To Neil Petersen for being a firebrand and an example of how to lead a church into prayer and revival. And William Marcellus Angellford for your generosity toward this project.

And to Wes Daughenbaugh, who mentored me in the anointing of the Holy Spirit, hiring me as a freshly graduated Bible college graduate all those years ago. For standing on the word of God and staying committed to the baptism with the Holy Spirit and having the sweetest spirit I have ever seen. It was an honor to serve under you before God called you back to the evangelistic ministry, and to be on your board. The world needs more anointed ministers like you that are unafraid to lay hands on people to receive the Holy Spirit in power. Thanks for writing the foreword to this book.

May more people's spiritual eyes be opened to the biblical truth of the baptism with the Holy Spirit through this book and receive the promised gift in Jesus' name!

## *Resources*

The Spirit Empowered Journal offers you life-changing steps that will enhance your Biblical and devotional studies.
This is an incredible, innovative approach to Bible study that will empower your spiritual journey.

*Available on Amazon*

Baby Boo Bear is going to the amusement park! But is he brave enough to ride the Dino-Saur? Find out in this thrilling adventure. Written by the Laskey kids with proceeds benefiting Middle East discipleship.

*Available on Amazon*

Adventures in the Spirit with Jared Laskey is a deep dive into the supernatural power of the Holy Spirit. This podcast is not just information, but impartation and activation so that you are empowered for your own adventures in the Spirit.

*Subscribe anywhere you listen to podcasts*

Be encouraged, equipped and empowered to live the supernatural, Spirit-empowered life. Receive profound revelation and deep Biblical insight in the Holy Spirit, prophecy, deliverance, healing, miracles, signs, wonders and more.

*Subscribe anywhere you listen to podcasts*

Made in the USA
Middletown, DE
31 March 2025